D0490730

C Collins

Easy Learning

French

Age 5-7

Je m'appelle _____ .
(My name is...)

J'ai _____ **ans.**
(I am...   ...years old.)

J'apprends le français!
(I'm learning French!)

How to use this book

- Find a quiet, comfortable place to work, away from other distractions.
- Tackle one topic at a time.
- Help with reading the instructions where necessary, and ensure that your child understands what to do.
- Help and encourage your child to check their own answers as they complete each activity.
- Discuss with your child what they have learnt.
- Let your child return to their favourite pages once they have been completed, to talk about the activities.
- Reward your child with plenty of praise and encouragement.
- Encourage your child to say the new words out loud. This will get them to practise speaking French, and help them to remember the new words.

Special Features

- Notes: these are divided into 'Tips' which give you tips about the language, 'Did you know...' which give you extra information about language and culture and 'Further learning' which suggest extra activities and encourages discussion with your child about what they have learnt.
- Not all French letters are pronounced the same as English letters and French words have a lot of silent letters (not pronounced). To help you, every time a new word or phrase is introduced, a pronunciation guide is given in square brackets, for example le **chat** [luh sha]. There are lots of hints in the tips sections to help you and your child learn how to say some of the more unusual sounds.
- Audio recordings of all the key vocabulary are available online at **www.collinslanguage. com/veryfirst**. Listen to the words and get your child to copy them and practise saying them. This will help you and your child to understand how the words are pronounced.

HarperCollins Publishers
Westerhill Road
Bishopbriggs
Glasgow
G64 2QT
Great Britain

First Edition 2010
Reprint 10 9 8 7 6 5 4 3 2 1 0
© HarperCollins Publishers 2010
ISBN 978-0-00-729886-0
www.collinslanguage.com
A catalogue record of this book is available from the British Library.
Printed and bound in China by South China Printing Co., Ltd

FOR THE PUBLISHERS
Rob Scriven
Gaëlle Amiot-Cadey
Genevieve Gerrard

CONTRIBUTORS
Jo Kentish
Helen Morrison

ILLUSTRATIONS AND TYPESETTING DESIGN
Q2AMedia

EARICH

Contents

Bonjour! Hello!

These two children have just met. Look at their conversation. Can you see two different greetings (hello and goodbye) and two questions and answers?

Bonjour!
(Hello!)

Comment tu t'appelles?
(What's your name?)

Je m'appelle Eve.
(My name's Eve.)

Bonjour!

Ça va?
(How are you?)

Oui, ça va bien, merci.
(I'm fine, thanks.)

Au revoir!
(Goodbye!)

Au revoir!

Bonjour [bongjoor]   **Comment tu t'appelles?** [komong too tapel]

Je m'appelle... [juh mapel]   **Ça va** [sa va]

Oui, ça va bien, merci [wee, sa va bien, merci]   **Au revoir** [oh ruhvwar]

My name is...

These two children are introducing themselves in French. Read the sentence under each picture. Now draw a picture of yourself in the empty box, say hello in French and write your name underneath.

Bonjour!
Je m'appelle Julie.

Bonjour!
Je m'appelle Marc.

_ _ _ _ _ _ _ _ _ _!

Je m'appelle _____ .

Did you know...?

In France people often shake hands or kiss on the cheeks when they greet each other.

Who's Who?

Play this game with a friend. Choose an identity for your friend from the characters below. They will have to guess what they are called by asking **Je m'appelle…?** "Am I called…?". Did they get it right? If they did, say **oui** [wee], which means "yes". If they didn't, say **non** [nong], which means "no".

Je m'appelle…?

Ziggy   **Bella**   **Nellie**   **Igor**   **Frosty**

Keep talking!

Two children are talking. Only one half of their conversation is written down. Fill in the missing greeting words and questions.

_____!   Bonjour!

_____?   Je m'appelle Luc.

_____?   Oui, ça va bien, merci.

_____!   Au revoir!

 **Further Learning**

Use puppets or your fingers to act out the conversation or find someone who can help you. Listen to the words on www.collinslanguage.com/veryfirst and practise saying the words out loud!

Les nombres
Numbers

Here are the numbers you need to count up to ten in French:

1	**2**	**3**	**4**	**5**
un	deux	trois	quatre	cinq
[ung]	[duh]	[trwa]	[katr]	[sank]
6	**7**	**8**	**9**	**10**
six	sept	huit	neuf	dix
[seess]	[set]	[weet]	[nuhf]	[deess]

Count in French

Look at these pictures and count the objects in French.
Write the number word in French under each picture.

q_____ _____ _____ _____

Tips. *qu sounds like "c" in "cat". You don't say the x on the end of deux – but you do say it on the end of six and dix. And at the end of six and dix, x sounds like "ss" in "mess"!*

How do you like them apples?

Look at the baskets. Read the number word underneath the basket and draw the right number of apples in each one. Now count the apples in each basket in French.

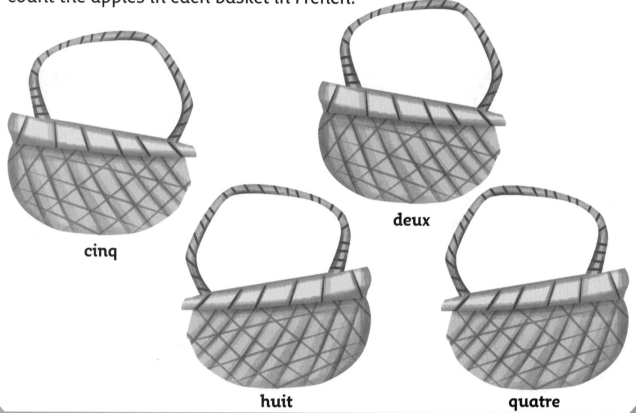

cinq

deux

huit

quatre

French sums

Can you do the sums, writing the answers in French?

quatre + deux = _____

sept + trois = _____

neuf – huit = _____

dix – six = _____

un + _____ = huit

cinq – _____ = deux

Further Learning

Practise counting in French at home using objects like pasta shapes or small toys. Can you count in different ways – odd and even numbers, loudly and quietly, backwards from ten?

Les couleurs
Colours

Follow the line from the paint pots and colour in the object.

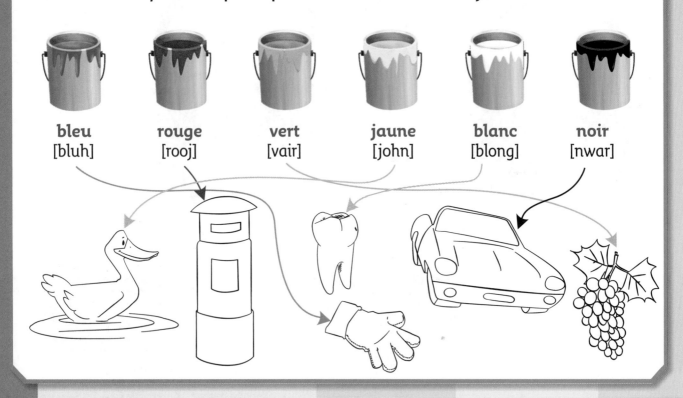

bleu	rouge	vert	jaune	blanc	noir
[bluh]	[rooj]	[vair]	[john]	[blong]	[nwar]

What colour is it?

Write the colour in French under the picture.
Count how many letters are in each one to help you.

_ _ _ _   _ _ _ _ _   _ _ _ _ _   _ _ _ _

Did you know...?

In France post boxes and post vans are yellow.

Colour the numbers!

Colour each number in the colour written underneath it.

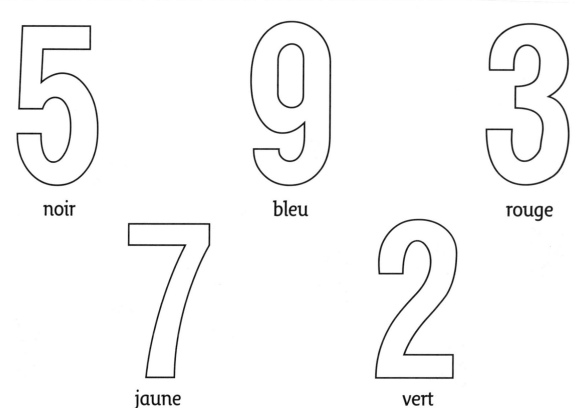

noir

bleu

rouge

jaune

vert

Can you remember how to say the numbers in French?

Match them up!

Match the picture on the left to the colour on the right.

•   • rouge

•   • jaune

•   • noir

•   • vert

Further Learning

Can you see any of these colours around you? Point to things near you and say what colour they are in French!

Ma famille
My family

Voici... [vwasee]

Marc is introducing his family.
Voici means "here is".

...ma **maman**
[ma mamong]

...ma **sœur**
[ma suhr]

...mon **papa**
[mong papa]

...ma **mamie**
[ma mamee]

...mon **frère**
[mong frair]

...mon **papi**
[mong papee]

Bonjour, ma famille!

Say hello to the family. The first one has been done for you.

Bonjour, papa!

Bonjour, _ _ _ _ _ _ !

Bonjour, _ _ _ _ _ _ !

Bonjour, _ _ _ _ _ !

Tips

Mon and ma both mean "my" in French. Look at the family members. Can you work out when you use mon and when you use ma?

Ma couleur préférée

Marc is talking about his family's favourite colours. Colour each person's outfit in their favourite colours. The word **aime** [em] means "likes".

"Mon **papa** aime le **rouge** et le **noir**."

"Mon **frère** aime le **jaune** et le **blanc**."

"Ma **maman** aime le **vert** et le **rouge**."

"Ma **sœur** aime le **noir** et le **bleu**."

Match them up!

These children are talking about their brothers and sisters. Read what they say and match each one to the pictures. **J'ai** [jay] means "I've got".

  J'ai un frère et deux sœurs. • •

J'ai deux frères. • •

 J'ai une sœur. • •

Further Learning

Can you say how many brothers and sisters you have? Notice that when you say "one sister", you use **une** [oon] instead of **un** to mean "one". To say you are an only child, you say **Je suis fils unique** [juh swee feess ooneek] if you are a boy, and **Je suis fille unique** [juh swee fee ooneek] if you are a girl.

11

Les animaux
Animals

Look at these animals:

le chien
[luh sheeang]

le chat
[luh sha]

le poisson
[luh pwasong]

le lapin
[luh lapang]

l'oiseau
[lwazoh]

le cheval
[luh shuhval]

l'araignée
[larenyay]

Make a list of the animals with the letter **a** in the word:

1 _____   2 _____   3 _____

4 _____   5 _____

Animal homes

Who lives in these homes? Match them up, write the missing words, and draw the missing pictures.

l'oiseau   _ '_ _ _ _ _ _ _ _   _ _ _ _ _ _ _ _   le chien

Tip *When a word begins with a vowel, like oiseau and araignée, le or la, meaning "the", is written as l'. Try and spot this when you learn more French words!*

Word search

Can you find six French animals in the square?

p	c	h	i	e	n	c
o	c	h	a	t	i	u
i	l	a	p	i	p	x
s	c	h	e	v	a	l
s	q	n	w	h	l	r
o	i	s	e	a	u	k
n	x	u	b	e	b	s

One animal is missing.
Which one is it? _____

Did you know...?

Dogs in French say *ouah ouah* [wa wa] and birds sing *cui cui* [kwee kwee] !

ouah ouah

cui cui

Quiz

Write your answers using the French words you have learnt so far.

1   Which animal lives in water? _____

2   Which animal is **noir**? _____

3   Can you name the animal that lives in a burrow? _____

4   Which animal has **huit** legs? _____

5   Which animal likes to chase le **chat**? _____

6   Which is bigger, l'**araignée** or le **cheval**? _____

Les vêtements
Clothes

Here are some words in French for clothes:

la **jupe**
[la joop]

la **chemise**
[la shuhmeez]

le **pantalon**
[luh pontalong]

le **pull**
[luh pool]

le **tee-shirt**
[luh tee-shairt]

les **chaussures**
[lay shohsoor]

les **chaussettes**
[lay shohset]

Quick quiz

Write your answers in French.

1 What do you wear when it is cold? _____

2 What do you wear on your feet? _____

3 Which clothes can you wear on your top half? _____

_____

4 Which of these clothes do you usually wear to school? _____

_____

Tip *In French the word for trousers is singular, so "one pair of trousers" is un pantalon. And the s on the plural words like chaussures and chaussettes is silent: you don't say it.*

Match them up!

Match the words to the picture on the left. Then draw yourself on the right, and match the words to what you're wearing.

- • la jupe •

- • les chaussettes •

- • les chaussures •

- • le tee-shirt •

- • la chemise •

- • le pantalon •

Draw yourself here.

Fill in the grid

Fill in the grid, using the French words for clothes.

1		h						t		
2							r			
3				–		h				
4			n							
5				m						
6			p							

Further Learning

Look again at the picture of the boy, and the picture you drew of yourself. Can you say what colours the clothes are in French?

15

La nourriture
Food

Here are some French words for things to eat:

la **pizza**
[la peetza]

la **glace**
[la glass]

le **sandwich**
[luh sondweech]

l'**orange**
[loronj]

les **frites**
[lay freet]

le **gâteau**
[luh gatoh]

la **pomme**
[la pom]

les **pâtes**
[lay pat]

What's on the list?

This shopping list has some missing letters.
Can you fill in the gaps and read the words?

l' _ ran _ _   l _ g _ _ ce   l _ _ fr _ _ _ s

le   gât _ _ u   la   _ om _ e   _ e _ p _ _ e _

Tip

Remember to put the "hat" ^ on the letter "a" when you write gâteau and pâtes.

Dinner time!

The plates are empty! Read what each child wants for dinner, and draw it onto the plates in front of them. One of the children has only thought of two things. Add another food item in the gap and draw it on the plate.

La pizza,	Le sandwich,	Les pâtes,
la pomme	l'orange	le gâteau
et les frites.	et la pomme.	et _____ .

Play a game!

Use dice to play this game. Look at the menu. Each item has a number. Take it in turns with a friend to throw the dice. When the dice is thrown, say the name and number of the food and circle it on the menu. Use a different colour each to circle the numbers. Whoever circles them all first is the winner!

Le menu
1 **la pizza**
2 **le sandwich**
3 **les frites**
4 **la pomme**
5 **la glace**
6 **le gâteau**

Further Learning

Some food words are written the same in English and French. Can you find them?

Dans ma trousse
In my pencil case

What's in your pencil case?

Follow the lines from the words to the pictures.
Then write the words under the pictures.

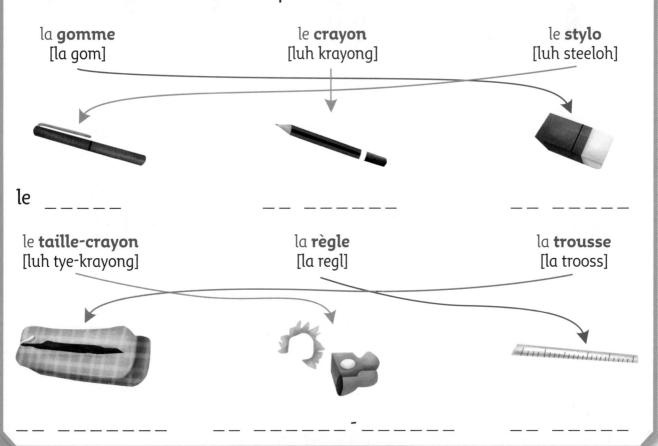

la **gomme**
[la gom]

le **crayon**
[luh krayong]

le **stylo**
[luh steeloh]

le _ _ _ _ _

_ _ _ _ _ _ _ _

_ _ _ _ _ _

le **taille-crayon**
[luh tye-krayong]

la **règle**
[la regl]

la **trousse**
[la trooss]

_ _ _ _ _ _ _ _ _

_ _ _ _ _ _ _ - _ _ _ _

_ _ _ _ _ _ _

Quick quiz

Answer the questions with the French words you have learned.

1   What do you use to draw a straight line? _____

2   Which two things can you use for writing? _____ et _____

3   Which item can you put all the others into? _____

4   Which item can you use to remove mistakes? _____

Tip *taille in taille-crayon rhymes with "pie" and "eye" in English.*

Play Kim's game

Get one of each of these items from your own pencil case and put them in a pile in front of you. Ask a friend to take one item away and hide it behind their back. Close your eyes while they do it – no peeking! Can you remember what they took away? Say the word in French.

How many?

Draw the correct number of items in each box.

huit crayons

cinq gommes

deux trousses

Try playing Kim's game with 6 pencils or crayons of different colours. Can you remember what colour your friend has taken away? Say the colour in French!

Qu'est-ce que tu aimes faire?
What do you like doing?

Here is how to say what you like doing in French:

J'aime...

[jem]

1 ...jouer au foot
[jooay oh foot]

2 ...lire
[leer]

3 ...jouer aux jeux vidéo
[jooay oh juh vidayoh]

4 ...danser
[donsay]

5 ...dessiner
[desseenay]

6 ...faire du vélo
[fair doo vayloh]

7 ...nager
[najay]

Look at the pictures and write what you think the hobby is in English.
Check your answers at the back of the book!

1 _____   2 _____   3 _____

4 _____   5 _____   6 _____

7 _____

Tip
The er ending on the verbs like jouer, danser, dessiner and nager has a silent r. Each of these verbs end in the sound 'ay'. If you want to practise saying these sentences, try doing an action at the same time to help you remember what they mean.

My hobbies

Choose two hobbies and draw yourself doing them.
Write what they are in French.

_____   _____

What I like

J'aime [jem] in French means "**I like...**"
So if you wanted to say "**I like** reading" you would say **J'aime lire**.
Now look at the list of hobbies.

Put a tick in the box if you like doing the hobby. Put a cross if you don't like doing it. Can you say out loud which ones you like doing?

J'aime....

faire du vélo ☐

nager ☐

jouer aux jeux vidéo ☐

jouer au foot ☐

danser ☐

dessiner ☐

Further Learning

If you **don't like** something you would say Je **n'aime pas** [juh nem pa]. So to say "I don't like dancing", you say Je n'aime pas danser. Look at where you ticked the boxes. Can you say which hobbies you like doing, and which you don't?

Tout sur moi
All about me

Draw a picture of yourself in the box. Fill in the gap underneath.

Je m'appelle _____

In the picture

What are you wearing? Give the names in French
of two things you are wearing in the picture.
Clothes are on pages 14–15.

_____ et _____ .

What colours have you used? Give the names in French of two colours you
have used in the picture. Colours are on pages 8–9.

_____ et _____ .

Tip

*If you get stuck on
this page, look back
through the book to
find the words.*

My family

Draw a picture of some people in your family.

Who have you drawn? Finish the sentence in French.
Family words are on pages 10–11.

Voici _____

_____

Further Learning

Can you say what the people in your family are wearing?

My favourite things

Write you favourite things in French.
Passe-temps [pass-tong] means "hobby". Remember
to write **le** or **la** before your favourite animal and food.

Ma **couleur** préférée, c'est le _____

Mon **passe-temps** préféré, c'est _____

Mon **animal** préféré, c'est _____

Ma **nourriture** préférée, c'est _____

Réponses
Answers

Page 4
My name is
Check your child's answer.

Page 5
Keep talking!
Bonjour!
Comment tu t'appelles?
Oui, ça va bien, merci.
Au revoir!

Page 6
Count in French
balloons – quatre
fish – sept
stars – dix
snails – huit

Page 7
How do you like them apples?

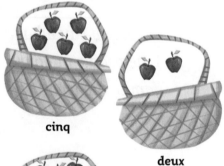

cinq

deux

huit

quatre

French sums
quatre + deux = <u>six</u>
sept + trois = <u>dix</u>
neuf – huit = <u>un</u>
dix – six = <u>quatre</u>
un + <u>sept</u> = huit
cinq – <u>trois</u> = deux

Page 8
Follow the lines
Check your child has coloured the objects in the right colours.

What colour is it?

b l e u   j a u n e

r o u g e   v e r t

Page 9
Colour the numbers

5 noir   **9** bleu   **3** rouge
7 jaune   **2** vert

Match them up!

rouge

jaune

noir

vert

Page 10
Bonjour, ma famille!
Bonjour, <u>m a m a n</u>!
Bonjour, <u>m a m i e</u>!
Bonjour, <u>p a p i</u>!

Tips
You use **mon** for boys and **ma** for girls.

Page 11
Ma couleur préférée
dad – red and black
brother – yellow and white
mum – green and red
sister – black and blue

Match them up!

J'ai un frère et deux sœurs.

J'ai deux frères.

J'ai une sœur.

Page 12
List of animals
1 chat
2 lapin
3 oiseau
4 cheval
5 araignée

Animal homes

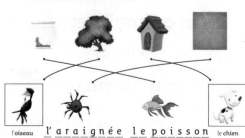

l'oiseau   l'araignée   le poisson   le chien